Contents

Alouette	36
Amazing Grace	41
Butcher Boy, The	40
Boys of Bluehill, The	46
Early One Morning	45
Drowsy Maggie	48
Galway Races, The	39
Go and Tell Aunt Rhody	37
Golden Jubilee, The	43
Harvest Home, The	47
I'll Tell Me Ma	28
Last Rose of Summer, The	32
Love Is Teasing	35
Minstrel Boy, The	29
Oh, Christmas Tree	44
Old MacDonald's Farm	23
On Top of Old Smoky	27
Oranges and Lemons	30
Planxty Irwin	38
Red River Valley	26
Roddy McCorley	42
Sally Gardens, The	24
Scarborough Fair	31
Spanish Lady, The	33
Whiskey in the Jar	34
Wild Rover, The	25

About This Booklet

This booklet gives you a carefully selected and of tunes suitable for the tin whistle with diagra fingering for each tune. It also contains some i basics of whistle playing and the rudiments of Not only will it make it easy for you to play the t also help you to learn to play from the written m a short time, you should be able to play tunes f only.

For those who are familiar with the tunes or who ca there is a twin pack containing a whistle and book who cannot read music or are not familiar with th is a triple pack which contains a whistle, booklet which you can listen to the tunes being pl accomplished player.

The best way of developing a style of your own is accomplished players and try to emulate aspects of their playing which appeal to you.

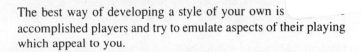

Order No. 1408
ISBN No. 1 85720 071 3

Copyright © 2001 Walton Manufacturing Ltd.

Walton Manufacturing Co. Ltd., Unit 6A, Rosemount Park Drive, Rosemount Business Park, Ballycoolin Road, Blanchardstown, Dublin 11, Ireland
USA Distributors: Walton Music Inc., P.O. Box 874, New York, NY 10009, U.S.A.

The Basics of Whistle Playing

HOLDING THE WHISTLE
Hold the whistle with the first three fingers of your left hand covering the three holes nearest the mouthpiece. The remaining three holes are covered with the first three fingers of your right hand.

The barrel of the whistle should rest on your thumbs. Place the mouthpiece between your lips making sure there is no contact between the mouthpiece and your teeth.

BLOWING
Breath control is one of the most important skills in whistle playing; it is also one of the most difficult. Blow softly for the lower notes, and harder for the higher notes. Rapid alteration between high notes and low notes is one of the most difficult skills to master on the tin whistle.

Continuous blowing is used for long notes or for smooth uninterrupted (legato) transition from note to note. To separate notes blow in a 'huh-huh' fashion. This is particularly useful for defining repeats of the same note. By using the tongue to go 'tuh-tuh', notes may be cut short thereby achieving a detached or staccato effect.

FINGERING
Cover the holes with the pads of your fingers not with the tips. Use only a gentle pressure.

Cover the holes completely. If air escapes through any gap between the pad of your finger and the hole, the sound will be shrill, squeaky or out ot pitch.

Learn to cover the holes from the top down i.e. cover the top hole first, then the top two, and so on, making sure you get a clean smooth sound. Do not lift your fingers too high off the whistle.

The diagrams under the music use black circles to indicate holes which are covered, and white circles to indicate holes which are not covered. Occasionally a hole must be half covered (see below). A + sign under the diagrams indicates that you must blow harder to achieve the higher notes.

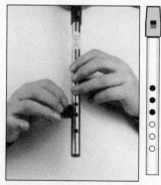

The black circles indicate notes which are covered.
The white circles indicate notes which are uncovered.
A hole which is half covered is indicated as shown here.

The Basics of Written Music

Music is written on five lines called a stave or staff. The stave is divided into bars or measures by vertical lines called barlines. Each measure contains a specific amount of music, specified by the time signature.

At the beginning of the stave is the G, or treble clef 𝄞. This indicates that the note on the second line from the bottom is the G above middle C on the piano.

Next is the key signature which indicates which notes are to be played sharp ♯ or flat ♭. The absence of a key signature indicates that no notes are to be played sharp or flat. On a piano, a sharp is the black note to the right of a white (natural ♮) note, and a flat is the black note to its left.

Where a note other than those indicated in the key signature is to be played, an accidental is used, i.e. a sharp, flat or natural sign is written before that note. Accidentals apply only to the measure in which they appear.

The time signature tells how many beats (upper number) and what type of beat (lower number) in each measure.

A Staff with Music

The key signature tells us that all F notes are to be played sharp. The time signature tells us that each measure must contain the equivalent of two quarter notes.

A dot after a note extends its time value by half. Tied notes are played as one note with the time value of the two. A rest is a silence. A repeat sign tells us to repeat the music from the beginning or from the preceeding repeat sign.

The Key of D

Since this booklet is for the D whistle, the only scales used are the scales of D major and G major. In the key of D the notes F and C are sharp as indicated by the key signature. The fingering for each note is shown by the diagrams under the notes. Memorise the fingering so that you will be able to finger the notes without looking at the diagrams. To play the high notes D′, E′ -etc. just blow a little harder. The + sign under the diagrams is to remind you of this.
Remember, black circles are fingered, white circles are not.

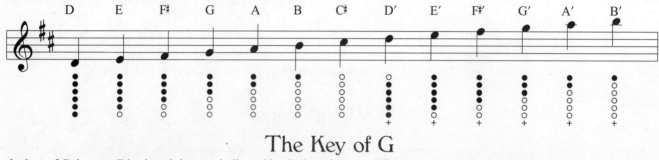

The Key of G

In the key of G the note F is played sharp as indicated by the key signature. The note C is played natural. The fingering for C natural is shown below. All the other notes are fingered as for the key of D.

The high C#′ and D′ do not feature in this booklet. They can sound piercing and shrill, and for that reason they are rarely used.

Notes and Rests

Notes are signs which represent musical sounds. The shape of the note shows its time value or how long it lasts. The position of the note on the stave shows its pitch i.e. how high or low it is. The most commonly used notes are shown below. Each of the groups of notes has the same time value – usually a count of four beats.

Rests are signs which represent musical silences. Each note has its equivalent silence as shown below.

Quavers and semiquavers can be joined or 'beamed' together in groups. The round part of a note is called the note head; the vertical part is called the stem; the curved part of quavers and semiquavers is called the tail or flag while the thick horizontal line which joins them together is called a beam. When notes are in the upper half of the stave they are usually upside down. This is a space-saving device so that they don't stick out too much. When quavers or semiquavers are inverted the tail or flag remains on the right of the stem.

Time Signatures

The most common time signatures are as follows.

$\frac{2}{4}$ has 2 quarter notes, or equivalent, in each measure. It is used in polkas and marches.

$\frac{3}{4}$ has 3 quarter notes, or equivalent, in each measure. It is used in old time waltzes.

$\frac{4}{4}$ has 4 quarter notes, or equivalent, in each measure. It is sometimes written as **C** ·which stands for common time, and is used in reels and hornpipes -etc.

$\frac{6}{8}$ has 6 eighth notes, or equivalent, in each measure. It is used in single and double jigs.

In Irish dance music $\frac{9}{8}$ is used for slip jigs and $\frac{12}{8}$ is used for slides.

TRIPLETS

A triplet is a group of three notes given the time value of two notes of the same type. The figure 3 is centred over or under the group and may also include a slur or a bracket.

Basic Techniques

Tongueing, slurring, cutting, sliding, trills and vibrato are techniques used in whistle playing. Slurring is used to describe continuous blowing of the whistle so that the notes glide into one another giving a smooth, flowing effect. Where notes are repeated the blowing must be interrupted, tongued or the repeating notes must be cut.

A note is cut by flicking a finger on a note higher than the one being played before playing it. As well as separating two identical notes cuts may be used to embellish or accentuate particular notes. A double cut is also used as a form of ornamentation. In this case the note being cut is sounded and then cut as above.

The example below shows a cut on the note F# and a duoble cut on the note A. The notes D, E, F, and G are usually cut with a flick on the A or fourth hole, while A and B can be cut with a flick on the C# or sixth hole. The note C# is not usually cut. The small notes used to indicate cuts are called grace notes.

Sliding is a technique used in slow tunes, where you slide up or down to a note by covering or uncovering the neighbouring note gradually by sliding your finger on to it or off it.

A trill or shake is used on sustained notes by rapid alteration between the note being played and the note above it.

Vibrato is used to modulate the pitch of a note. This is done by waving a finger alongside the hole being played to make the note vibrate or wobble or by covering and uncovering a hole below the one being played.

In Irish traditional music it is not usual to annotate decorations and embellishments in detail as it is left to the player to decide how a tune should be interpreted.

Die Grundlagen des Tin Whistlespiels

DAS HALTEN DER TIN WHISTLE
Halte die Tin Whistle mit den ersten drei Fingern der linken Hand. Decke damit die obersten drei Löcher ab. Die unteren Löcher werden mit den ersten drei Fingern der rechten Hand abgedeckt.
Das Rohr der Tin Whistle liegt auf beiden Daumen. Das Mundstück befindet sich zwischen deinen Lippen. Achte darauf, dass du damit nicht die Zähne berührst.

DAS BLASEN
Die Atemkontrolle ist eine der wichtigsten, aber auch schwersten Techniken des Tin Whistlespielens. Bei den tieferen Tönen musst du sachte blasen, und bei den höheren Tönen etwas fester. Schnelle und abrupte Wechsel zwischen tiefen und hohen Tönen gehören zu den schwersten Techniken der Tin Whistle.
Bei langen Tönen, oder gebundenen (legato) Melodiepassagen musst du langanhaltend blasen.
Um Töne voneinander zu trennen, benutzt man die 'Huh-huh'-Blastechnik. Die ist hilfreich, wenn man ein und denselben Ton mehrmals hintereinander wiederholen muss.
Wenn du kurze, gestossene Töne spielen willst, benutzt du deine Zunge für den 'Tuh-tuh'-Effekt (Stakkato).

DIE GRIFFTECHNIK
Decke die Löcher nicht mit den Fingerspitzen, sondern den Fingerballen ab. Wende dabei nur wenig Druck an. Schliesse die Löcher vollständig. Wenn Luft zwischen deinen Fingerballen und dem Flötenloch durchkommt, klingen die Töne schrill und falsch.
Wenn du die Löcher greifst, beginne mit dem obersten Loch, dann folgt das Zweite von oben usw. Achte darauf, dass du saubere, klare Töne spielst. Die Finger dürfen sich nicht zu weit von den Flötenlöchern entfernen.
In den Griffbildern unter den Noten stehen schwarze Punkte für gegriffene und weisse Punkte für offene Locher. Gelegentlich werden Löcher halbgeschlossen (siehe unten). A+ unter einem Griffbild bedeutet, das du fester blasen musst, um die hohen Töne zu bekommen.

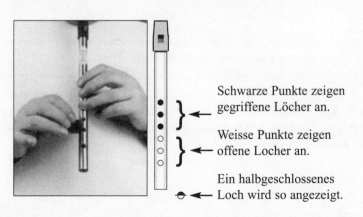

Schwarze Punkte zeigen gegriffene Löcher an.

Weisse Punkte zeigen offene Locher an.

Ein halbgeschlossenes Loch wird so angezeigt.

Einführung in das Notenlesen

Musik wird in einem Notensystem von fünf Linien notiert. Es wird durch vertikale Linien -die Taktstriche- in verschiedene Takte unterteilt. Innerhalb jeden Taktes befindet ein kleiner Musikabschnitt, der durch die Taktart bestimmt wird.

Am Anfang des Notensystems befindet sich der Notenschlüssel, entweder ein G, oder ein Violinschlüssel. Das bedeutet, dass die Note auf der zweiten unteren Linie das G über dem mittleren C auf den Klavier ist. Dann folgt die Tonartbezeichnung, die bestimmt welche Töne erhöht ♯ oder erniedrigt ♭ werden. Wenn keine Vorzeichen angegeben sind, bedeutet dies, das keine Töne erhöht oder erniedrigt werden. Auf dem Klavier ist ein erhöhter Ton eine schwarze Taste direkt rechts von einer weissen Taste, und ein erniedrigter Ton liegt direkt links von einer weissen Taste.

Manchmal kommen erhöhte oder erniedrigte Noten nicht in der Tonartbezeichnung am Anfang des Notensystems vor, sondern mitten im Notentext. Diese Vorzeichen gelten dann nur für den Takt in dem sie stehen, und sonst nicht.

Die Taktart gibt an, wieviel Hauptschläge (Zählzeiten) in einem Takt vorkommen (obere Zahl) und um welche Art von Zählzeit es sich handelt (untere Zahl).

Das Notensystem

Dieses Tonartzeichen besagt, dass alle F-Töne um einen halben Ton zu Fis erhöht werden.Die Taktart besagt, dass sich alle Takte aus dem Equivalent von zwei Viertelnoten zusammensetzen.Ein Punkt nach einer Note verlängert sie um die Hälfte ihres Wertes. Bei der gebundenen Note verdoppelt sich der Wert.Bei der Pause spielt man nicht.Ein Wiederholungszeichen bedeutet, dass der Musikabschnitt vom Anfang oder dem vorhergehenden Wiederholungszeichen an, nochmal gespielt wird.

Die Tonart D-dur

Diese Ausgabe ist für die D-Flöte, und deswegen spielen wir hier nur in den Tonarten D-dur und G-dur.
In der Tonart D-dur werden die Töne F und C durch Vorzeichen zu Fis und Cis erhöht.
Unter den Noten befinden sich die Griffbilder. Lerne alle Griffe auswendig, sodass du beim Spielen nicht mehr auf die Griffbilder schauen musst. Wenn du die hohen Töne D′ und E′ -usw. spielst, musst du fester blasen. Das ist die Bedeutung des + Zeichens unter den Griffbildern. Und wie gesagt, schwarze Punkte stehen für gegriffene, und die weissen für offene Löcher.

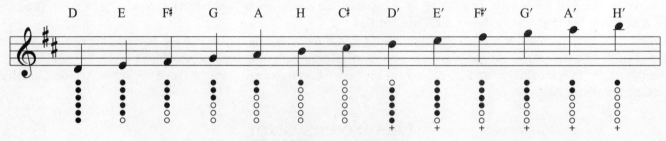

Die Tonart G-dur

In der Tonart G-dur wird das F durch Vorzeichen zu Fis erhöht. Der Ton C wird nicht erhöht. Das folgende Griffbild zeigt dir die Griffweise für C. Alle anderen Töne werden genauso gegriffen, wie in der Tonart D-dur.

Das hohe Cis′ und das hohe D kommen in diesem Heft nicht vor. Sie können sehr schrill und durchdringend klingen, und darum werden sie nur selten benutzt.

Pour Commencer à Jouer du flûteau

POUR TENIR LE FLÛTEAU

Tenir le flûteau à l'aide de la main gauche. Couvrir de haut en bas les trois premiers trous près de l'embouchoir, à l'aide des trois premiers doigts, c'est-à-dire, avec l'index, le majeur et l'annulaire. De la même façon, couvrir les trois autres trous restants avec les trois doigts de la main droite.

Le cylindre du flûteau se repose sur les deux pouces. Placer l'embouchoir ou bec entre les lévres en évitant tout contact avec les dents.

POUR SOUFFLER

Il est essentiel de contrôler le souffle pour jouer de cet instrument, ce qui n'est pas toujours facile. Il faut souffler doucement pour produire les notes graves. Souffler plus fort pour obtenir les notes aiguës.

Le plus difficile au flûteau est d'alterner entre note grave et note aiguë, en changeant rapidement de l'une à l'autre.

On fait un souffle continu pour les notes longues et pour passer d'une note à une autre de façon lisse et sans interruption. C'est ce qu'on appelle legato.

Pour séparer les notes, on souffle comme pour dire 'heu-heu'. Cette manière est très utile pour produire les notes répétées. Avec la langue, faire un mouvement 'tou-tou' pour faire des notes très courtes qu'on appelle 'piquées' ou staccato.

LE DOIGTÉ

Utiliser la pulpe du doigt pour couvrir le trou. Ne pas utiliser le bout du doigt. Il suffit d'appuyer doucement. Bien couvrir le trou de façon compléte. Si jamais l'air peut s'échapper entre le doigt et le trou, on entendra un son trés perçant et désagréable. Commencer en couvrant les trous toujours du haut vers le bas. Vérifier d'abord la note produite en couvrant le premier trou en haut, ensuite celle obtenue en couvrant les deux premiers trous et ainsi de suite. Chercher à produire toujours un son bien net et continu. Ne soulevez pas trop les doigts du flûteau. Dans le tableau en dessous de chaque note, les ronds noirs indiquent qu'il faut couvrir trous. Les blancs signifient qu'il faut laisser ces trous ouverts. Parfois, il est nécessaire de couvrir un trou seulement à moitié. (voir ci-dessous) Le signe + indique qu'il faut souffler plus fort pour produire la note plus aiguë.

Les ronds noirs indiquent les trous à couvrir.

Les ronds blancs indiquent les trous à laisser ouverts.

Un trou à moitié couvert est indiqué à l'aide de ce signe.

Les Bases Du Solfége

Les notes de musique s'écrivent sur cinq lignes horizontales qu'on appelle la portée. A l'aide de lignes verticales, on divise la portée en mesures. A gauche de la portée, le signe 𝄞 marque la clef de sol: la deuxième ligne horizontale en montant est donc la note de sol, c'est-à-dire sur un clavier, celle qui est au-dessus du do au milieu. L'armure indique les notes qui sont dièses ♯ ou bémols ♭. L'absence d'armure signifie qu'aucune note sur la portée est dièse ou bémol. Le dièse ♯ signifie un demi-ton plus aigu: pour le clavier d'un piano, par exemple, il faut jouer la touche noire à droite ou la blanche la plus proche à droite. Le signe ♮ signifie bécarre: au piano, c'est le plus souvent une touche blanche simplement. Le signe ♭ bémol signifie qu'il faut jouer un demi-ton plus grave; au piano, le plus souvent, c'est la touche noire à gauche. Si la note n'est pas marquée à l'aide de l'armure au début mais seulement au cours du morceau, elle s'appelle un accident, et dans ce cas-là, la valeur du signe dièse, bémol ou bécarre ne dure que pour la mesure où ce signe se trouve.

Le chiffre indicateur indique pour chaque mesure le temps (chiffre en haut) et la valeur des notes (chiffre en bas).

La Portée Avec Des Notes De Musique

L'armure dans ce cas-ci nous indique que tous les fa doivent être joués fa dièse.
Le chiffre indicateur signifie que chaque mesure doit avoir deux noires ou leur équivalent (quatre croches, une blanche...).
Un point après la note (note pointée) signifie que doit s'ajouter la moitié de sa valeur normale.
Une liaison relie deux notes qui se jouent comme une seule note ayant la valeur des deux.
Une pause signifie un silence.
Le signe reprise indique qu'il faut reprendre tout soit depuis le début soit depuis le dernier signe de reprise.

Ton De Re Majeur

Cette méthode est conçue pour le fluteau en *ré* majeur. C'est pourquoi elle n'utilise que les tonalités de re majeur et de *sol* majeur. En *ré* majeur, les notes *fa* et *do* sont dièses comme l'indique l'armure. Le petit schéma en dessous de chaque note indique le doigté pour chacun des six trous. En mémorisant ce doigté au début, vous pourrez bientôt dispenser des schémas pour lire directement chaque note sur la portée. Pour jouer les notes plus aigües, ré', mi'..., il suffit de suffler un peu plus fort à chaque fois que vous voyez le signe + qui vous servira de rappel. Attention: il faut couvrir les cercles noirs et non pas les cercles blancs.

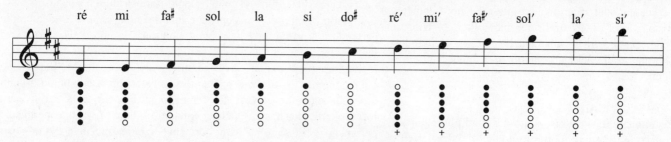

Ton De Sol Majeur

En *sol* majeur, le *fa* est toujours dièse comme l'indique l'armure de cette tonalité. Le *do* ne l'est pas, et nécessite un doigté différent comme ci-dessous. Toutes les autres notes restent les mêmes comme pour la tonalité de *ré* majeur.

Les notes les plus aigües, *do*# et *Re'* ne figurent pas dans cette méthode. Elles peuvent donner un son trop perçant et désagréable et ne sont donc utilisées que rarement.

Istruzioni fondamentali per suonare il Tin Whistle

COME SOSTENERE IL FLAUTO
Sostenere il flauto con le prime tre dita della mano sinistra coprendo i primi tre fori vicino all'imboccatura. I tre fori restanti sono coperti dalle prime tre dita della mano destra.
La canna del flauto deve essere morbidamente sostenuta tra i polpastrelli dei due pollici. Posizionare l'imboccatura tra le labbra della bocca assicurandosi che non ci sia nessun contatto tra l'imboccatura ed i denti.

COME SOFFIARE
Per suonare il Tin Whistle uno dei punti più importanti e anche più difficili è proprio il controllo del fiato. Per le note basse bisogna soffiare dolcemente e più forte per quelle alte. I cambiamenti veloci tra note alte e basse sono una parte molto difficile da imparare e da eseguire poi con il Tin Whistle.
Un soffio continuo viene usato per le note lunghe o per una legatura, cioè l'intervallo non interrotto tra nota e nota.
Per separare le note si consiglia di soffiare con uno stile 'huh-huh'. Questa tecnica è particolarmente utile per ripetere due note uguali.
Usando invece la lingua facendo 'tuh-tuh', le note vengono tagliate e si produce un effetto di staccato.

COME COPRIRE I FORI
Coprire i fori completamente con una leggera pressione dei polpastrelli e non con la punta delle dita. Se dovesse fuoriuscire dell'aria negli interstizi tra dita e fori, il suono prodotto sarà stridulo e stonato.
È importante imparare a coprire i fori da cima a fondo, ad esempio partendo dal primo foro su in cima, continuando con il secondo e così via, assicurandosi che il suono sia nitido e pulito. Ricordarsi di non alzare le dita troppo distanti dal flauto. Si può notare che in questo libro vi sono dei diagrammi di punti e cerchi sotto la musica di ciascun brano. I punti neri indicano i fori coperti ed i cerchi (punti bianchi) indicano invece i fori scoperti, cioè aperti. Qualche volta un foro dovrà essere coperto solo per metà (vedi sotto). Alcuni fori sono contrassegnati con un + per indicare che quella nota deve essere suonata in un'ottava più alta.

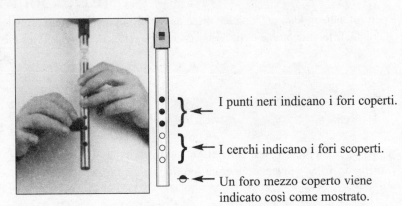

I punti neri indicano i fori coperti.

I cerchi indicano i fori scoperti.

Un foro mezzo coperto viene indicato così come mostrato.

Nozioni Di Base Della Musica Scritta

La musica viene scritta su cinque linee chiamate pentagramma o rigo musicale. Il pentagramma viene a sua volta suddiviso in tante piccole parti denominate battute o misure con delle linee verticali chiamate stanghette. Ogni misura contiene una parte musicale di uguale durata, contrassegnata dal tempo musicale (un segno speciale detto chiave).

All'inizio del pentagramma c'è il SOL o Chiave di violino 𝄞 ad indicare che la nota sulla seconda linea è SOL sopra il DO dominante del piano. Subito dopo la chiave si trovano le eventuali alterazioni musicali costanti che indicano quali sono le note che dovranno essere suonate in diesis o in bemolle. Se non vi sono delle alterazioni le note non verranno suonate nè in diesis ♯ e nè in bemolle ♭. Nel pianoforte un diesis è la nota nera sul lato destro di una bianca (bequadro ♮), mentre un bemolle è una nota nera sul suo lato sinistro. Possono però anche sussistere delle alterazioni musicali momentanee quando si trovano nelle diverse battute davanti alle note e valgono solo per la misura dove sono segnate. Il tempo musicale dice quanti battiti (numero sopra la frazione) e che tipo di battiti (numero sotto la frazione) sono presenti in una misura.

Un pentagramma con la musica

Qui sopra l'alterazione indica che tutte le note FA sono in diesis. Il tempo musicale è di 2/4 e quindi ogni misura dovrà contenere il valore delle note equivalente a 2/4. Un punto posto a destra di una nota o di una pausa ne aumenta il valore della sua metà e perciò prende il nome di punto di valore. La linea curva che si pone sotto (o sopra) due o più note dello stesso nome e della stessa altezza si chiama legatura di valore e serve a prolungare il suono della prima nota aggiungendovi il valore delle altre; si suona una nota con il valore delle due note legate. Una pausa è un silenzio.

Un segno di ripetizione indica che la musica deve essere ripetuta dall'inizio del brano o dal segno di ripetizione precedente.

La Chiave Di Re

Dato che questo libretto è per il Whistle in RE, le uniche scale usate sono la scala di RE e di SOL maggiore. In chiave di RE le note FA e DO sono contrassegnate da due alterazioni diesis accanto alla chiave di violino. Il movimento delle dita per ogni nota viene mostrato nel diagramma qui di seguito riportato sotto le note. Si consiglia di memorizzare il diagramma per essere così in grado di suonare senza guardarlo. Per suonare le note alte RE, MI, ecc. è sufficiente soffiare più forte ed il segno + sotto il diagramma sta a ricordarne proprio questo. Ricordare che i punti neri sono i fori coperti sul flauto ed i cerchi i fori aperti.

La Chiave Di Sol

In chiave di SOL il FA è suonato in diesis come indicato dall'alterazione. Il DO è bequadro perché naturale. Il movimento delle dita per suonare il DO naturale è qui indicato. Tutte le altre note si suonano come in chiave di RE.

Il DO# diesis alto e il RE' non compaiono in questo libretto. Hanno un suono pungente e stridulo e proprio per questo motivo si usano raramente.

Instrucciones básicas para tocar el Tin Whistle

SOSTENER LA FLAUTA

Sostener la flauta con los tres primeros dedos de la mano izquierda, cubriendo los tres primeros agujeros cercanos a la embocadura. Luego los tres agujeros restantes serán cubiertos con los tres primeros dedos de la mano derecha.

El cuerpo de la flauta debe ahora estar reposando en ambos pulgares. Poner la embocadura entre los labios.

No debe haber contacto entre la embocadura y los dientes.

SOPLADO

El control de la respiración es uno de los más importantes requisitos para tocar el Tin Whistle y al mismo tiempo uno de los más difíciles.

Los cambios bruscos entre las notas altas y bajas son unas de las técnicas más difíciles de realizar en el Tin Whistle.

Un soplado constante se utiliza para las notas largas o para ligaduras entre una nota y otra.

Para separar las notas sople de una manera huh-huh, éste sistema de soplado es muy útil para definir repeticiones de una misma nota.

Soplando de una manera tuh-tuh, usando la lengua, se producen sonidos cortos y muy definidos obteniéndose así un efecto staccato.

CUBRIR LOS AGUJEROS

Cubrir los agujeros presionando ligeramente con las yemas pero no con las puntas de los dedos. Cubrir los agujeros completamente, si el aire sale a través de alguna rendija el sonido sera chilloso o desafinado.

Aprender a cubrir los agujeros de arriba a abajo, por ejemplo, cubrir el primer agujero luego los dos primeros y así sucesivamente asegurándose de obtener un sonido suave y claro. No aleje demasiado los dedos de la flauta. Los diagramas debajo de los temas utilizan círculos negros para indicar que los agujeros deben ser cubiertos completamente por los dedos y los círculos blancos indican que no deben ser cubiertos.

En algunos casos los agujeros deben ser cubiertos sólo en su mitad (ver dibujo) un + debajo de los diagramas indica que se debe incrementar la presión del aire para obtener notas de una octava más alta.

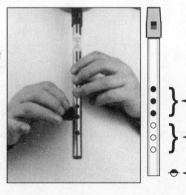

} ← Los círculos negros indican los agujeros que deben ser cubiertos.

} ← Los círculos blancos indican los agujeros que no deben ser cubiertos.

← Un agujero cubierto en su mitad debe hacerce así.

Lo básico de la música escrita

La música se escribe sobre cinco lineas horizontales llamado pentagrama. El pentagrama se sub-divide en compases por medio de lineas verticales. Cada compás contiene una parte de la música de igual duración indicada por la signatura de compás. Al inicio del pentagrama se encuentra la clave de sol 𝄞. Éste indica que la nota de la segunda linea es SOL sobre el DO dominante en el piano. Luego está la armadura que indica cuales notas deben ser tocadas de forma sostenida ♯ o bemol ♭. La ausencia de la armadura indica que las notas no deben ser tocadas ni en forma sostenida ni bemol. En el piano, el sostenido es el teclado negro ubicado a la derecha del blanco(nota sin alteración) y el bemol es el teclado negro a la izquierda del mismo. Cuando una nota debe ser tocada de manera diferente a aquellas indicadas en la armadura, se utiliza un accidente. Por ejemplo un símbolo de sostenido o bemol debe estar escrito delante de la nota natural ♮.
Los accidentales afectan solamente al compás en el cual se ubican.
La signatura de compás indica la cantidad de golpes (en el dividendo) y el tipo de golpe (en el divisor) en cada compás.

Un pentagrama musical.

En el pentagrama de arriba la armadura indica que todas las notas FA deben ser tocadas en sostenido.
La signatura de compás indica que cada compás debe ser equivalente a dos cuartos.
El punto después de la nota indica la prolongación de su tiempo en un medio más. Las notas ligadas se tocan como si fueran una nota con el valor del tiempo de dos notas. Un silencio es una pausa.
El símbolo de repetición indica repetir la musica desde el inicio o desde el previo punto de repetición.

La Clave De Re

Devido a que éste folleto es para la clave de RE, las únicas escalas usadas son las de RE mayor y SOL mayor. En la escala de RE las notas FA y DO son sostenidas porque así lo indica la signatura de compás La posición de los dedos para cada nota está demostrada a través de los diagramas debajo de las notas. La memorización de la posición de los dedos es fundamental para tocar cada nota sin necesidad de mirar los diagramas. Para tocar las notas altas RE, MI, etc, basta incrementar la presión del soplado. El signo + debajo de los diagramas servirá para recordar esto. Recordemos que los círculos negros deben ser cubiertos.

La Clave De Sol

En la clave de SOL la nota FA se toca en sostenido tal como indica la signatura de compás.
La nota DO se toca de manera natural o becuadro.
La pocisión de los dedos para la nota DO está demostrada en el dibujo más abajo. El resto de las notas se tocan en clave de RE

El DO#′ sostenido mayor y RE′ mayor no aparecen en éste folleto. Pues pueden sonar chilloso o desafinado, y por esta razón son raramente usados.

たて笛演奏の基礎

たて笛の持ち方

たて笛を左手で持ち、マウスピースに近い3つの穴を人差し指、中指、薬指で押さえます。残りの3つの穴は、右手の人差し指、中指、薬指で押さえます。

笛筒は、両親指で支えられている状態です。

マウスピースを唇に当てます。歯に当たらないよう気を付けてください。

吹き方

息の吐き出し方は、たて笛を吹く際の重要なポイントの1つであり、難しいポイントでもあります。低い音を出すにはやさしく吹き、高い音を出すには強く吹きます。1オクターブを超える音程間で小刻みに変化を付けるには高度な技術が必要であり、たて笛を習得する上で最も難しいテクニックの1つと言えます。

続けて吹くことにより、長い音を出したり、音程間で途切れることなく（レガート）滑らかな旋律を演奏したりします。

一音ずつ切るには、「フー、フー」と言うようなつもりで吹きます。この方法は、特に同じ音を区切るときに便利です。

舌を使って「トゥ、トゥ」と言うようなつもりで吹くことにより、音を短く区切ったりスタッカート効果を出したりすることができます。

指使い

指先でなく、指たぶで穴を塞ぎます。軽く押さえるようにしてください。

穴を完全に塞ぎます。指たぶと穴との間の隙間から空気が漏れると、甲高いキーキーいう音になったり、音が外れたりします。

上から順に穴を押さえるよう練習してください。つまり、一番上の穴を最初に押さえてからその下の穴、といった順番で押さえ、はっきりとした滑らかな音が出ることを確認します。

たて笛から指を離すときは、指を高く上げ過ぎないようにします。

楽譜の下の図には、押さえる穴を黒で、押さえない穴を白で示しています。

場合によっては、穴を半分押さえる必要があります（下図を参照）。穴に「+」が記されている場合は、その音を強く吹いて1オクターブ高くすることを示しています。

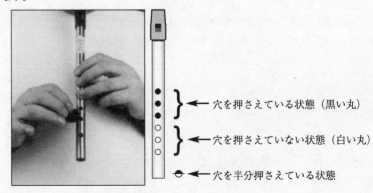

楽譜の基礎

楽譜は、5線上に書き込まれます。この5線は、縦線（小節線）で小節に分割されます。

5線譜の初めに、Gまたはト音記号が記入されます。これは、下から2番目の線がピアノの中央にある「ド」から上がった最初の「ソ」になることを示しています。

次に記入される調号は、シャープ（♯）またはフラット（♭）を付ける音符を示しています。調号が付いていない場合、どの音符にもシャープ（♯）またはフラット（♭）を付けないことを表します。ピアノでは、シャープは白い鍵盤（ナチュラル：♮）の右にある黒い鍵盤で、半音高い音になります。フラットは左の黒い鍵盤で、半音低い音になります。調号が示している音以外を表す場合は、その音符の前に臨時記号としてシャープ、フラット、またはナチュラルを付けます。

臨時記号は、その小節にのみ適用されます。

拍子記号は、小節内に含まれる音符の数（上の数字）と音符の種類（下の数字）を表しています。

楽譜の構成

この調号は、すべての「ファ」にシャープを付けることを表しています。この拍子記号は各小節に4分音符が2つ含まれることを示しています。音符の後ろの付点は、その音符が半音長いことを示しています。タイでつながれた音符は、その音符2つ分の長さになります。

リピート記号は、最初から繰り返すか、その前に記されたリピート記号から繰り返すことを表しています。

ニ長調

この入門書は、ニ長調のたて笛用であるため、すべての楽譜はニ長調またはト長調で書かれています。各音の指使いが音符の下に図解されています。図を見ずにその音を出すことができるよう、各音の指使いを覚えてください。1オクターブ高い「レ」や「ミ」を出すには、強めに吹きます。この場合、図の下に「+」が記されています。黒い丸は押さえる穴、白い丸は押さえない穴を示しています。

ト長調

ト長調では、調号で示されているように「ファ」にシャープが付きます。「ド」はナチュラルです。ナチュラルの「ド」の指使いが下図に示されています。その他の音の指使いは、ニ長調と同じです。

1オクターブ高い「ド♯」と「レ」は、この入門書では、表記されません。これらの音は甲高いキーキーいう音になるため、めったに使われません。

Old MacDonald's Farm

The Sally Gardens

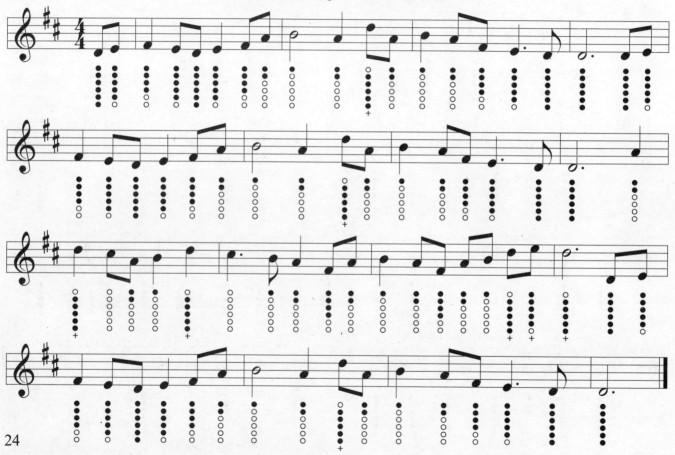

The Wild Rover

Red River Valley

On Top of Old Smoky

I'll Tell Me Ma

The Minstrel Boy

Oranges and Lemons

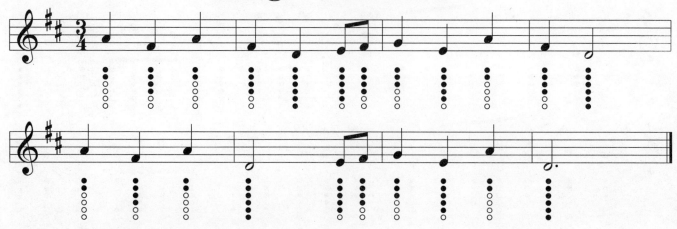

Scarborough Fair

The Last Rose of Summer

The Spanish Lady

Whiskey in the Jar

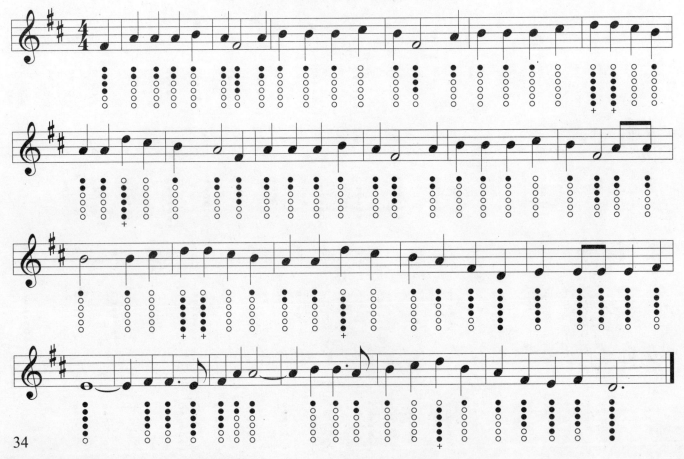

Love Is Teasing

35

Alouette

Go and Tell Aunt Rhody

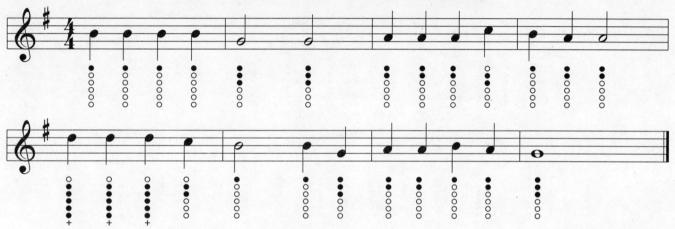

Planxty Irwin

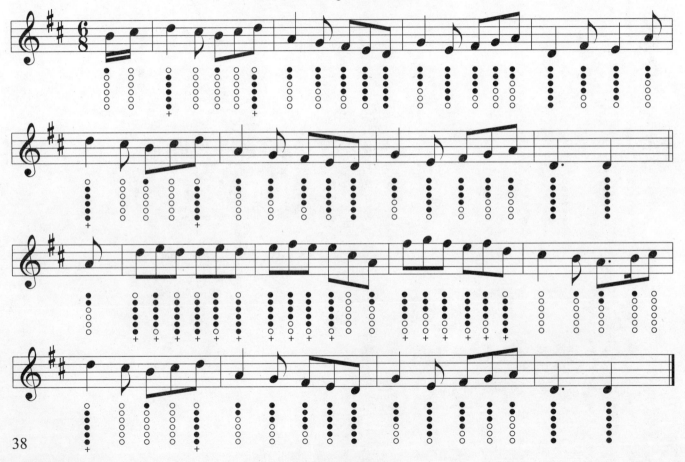

The Galway Races

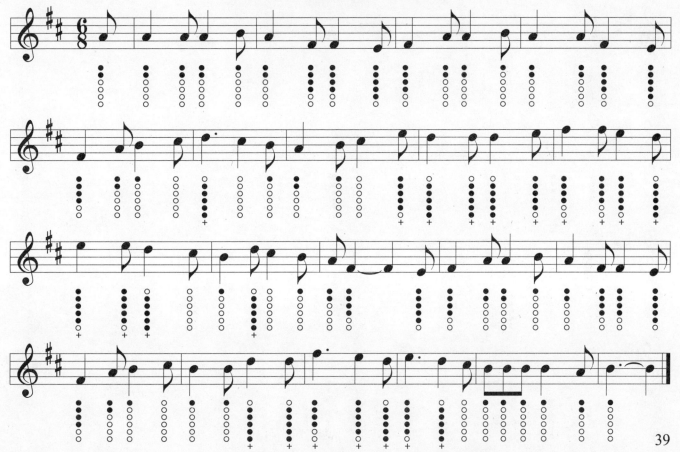

The Butcher Boy

Amazing Grace

Roddy McCorley

The Golden Jubilee

Oh, Christmas Tree

Early One Morning

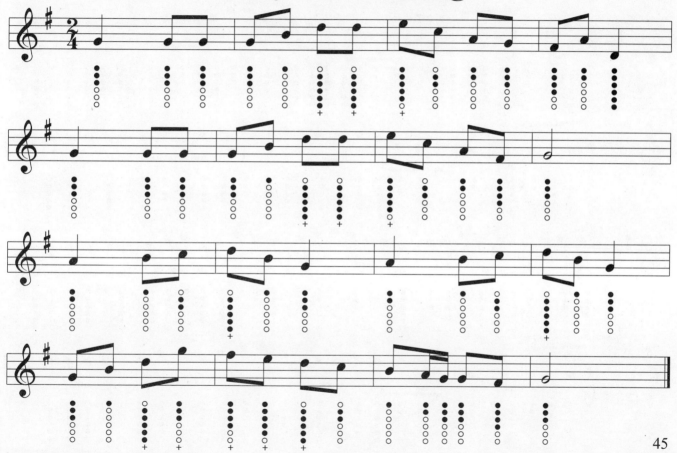

The Boys of Bluehill

The Harvest Home

Drowsy Maggie

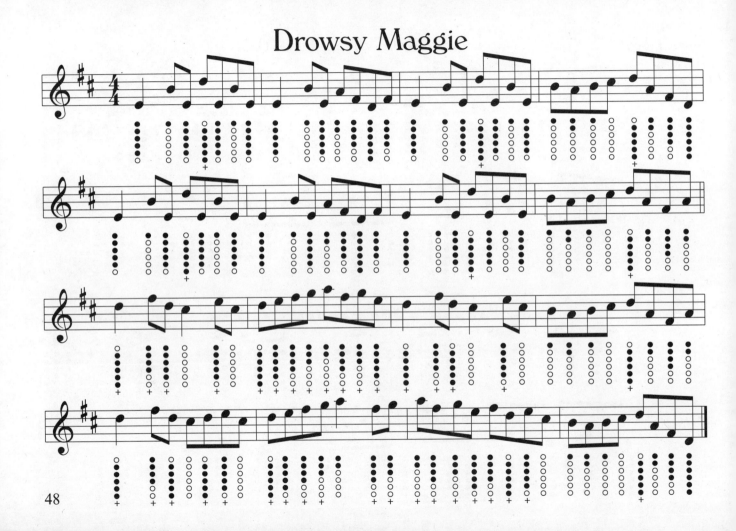